ISSUES IN OUR WORLD

FAIR TRADE

Adrian Cooper

Aladdin / Watts
London • Sydney

ABOUT THIS BOOK

FAIR TRADE is an issue that affects us all. This book will help you to learn about trade. Find out why trade can sometimes be unfair. Look at the effects of trade around the world. You will also find out about organisations that try to make trade fairer.

© Aladdin Books Ltd 2007
Produced by Aladdin Books Ltd
2/3 Fitzroy Mews, London W1T 6DF

ISBN 978–07496–7488–5

First published in 2007 by

Franklin Watts	Franklin Watts Australia
338 Euston Road	Level 17/207 Kent Street
London NW1 3BH	Sydney NSW 2000

Franklin Watts is a division of Hachette Children's Books.

Designers: Flick, Book Design and Graphics Simon Morse
Editors: Harriet Brown / Katie Dicker
Picture Researcher: Brian Hunter Smart
The author, Adrian Cooper, is an author and filmmaker who has worked in East Africa, India and, for Channel 4 and the BBC, in the UK.
The consultant, Rob Bowden, is an education consultant, author and photographer specialising in social and environmental issues.

A CIP catalogue record for this book is available from the British Library.

Dewey Classification: 382'.71

CONTENTS

INTRODUCTION

Today, our food, clothes and television programmes are all part of our lives because of trade. When trade is fair, it helps to improve standards of living. But trade can also be unfair. What is fair trade? Why is some trade unfair? What can be done about it?

In some parts of the world, children are forced to work in terrible conditions.

Today, it is easier than ever to communicate and trade with people all over the world.

WORLD TRADE

Today, we can travel across the world very easily. Telephones and computers also help us to work with people in other countries.

The world is constantly changing. We no longer have to get our food from a local farmer. Food can be transported so it arrives fresh from anywhere in the world. Some companies now choose to work in certain countries because they can save money.

THE HISTORY OF TRADE

People have always traded with each other. In Roman times, silk was transported 6,500 km from China to Europe along the old 'Silk Road'. Wool, gold and silver were taken from Europe into China. Swahili and Arabic traders also used the Indian Ocean and the Red Sea. Their boats carried spices and precious stones from Asia to Africa and then on to Arabia.

Trade has helped countries and groups of people to develop.

TRADE WORDS

Trade – To exchange, buy or sell.
Goods – Things that are made, farmed or mined, such as diamonds.
Service – Something that is provided, such as healthcare.
Imports/Exports – Goods or services that arrive from (or are sent to) another country.

Judging fairness

How do we measure the fairness of trade when we buy something? We may discover that the people who made a new mobile phone were treated badly. But these people may have been worse off if they did not have a job at all.

Today, people, companies and governments are all involved in trade and have to judge how fair they think trade is.

5

Mobile phones

Mobile phones contain materials, such as plastics and metals. These come from many different parts of the world. The parts travel a long way to become phones in your local shop.

THE IMPORTANCE OF FAIR TRADE

For one-fifth of the world's population, shelter, safe water and food are not available.

Poverty is not just about money. Poverty is also about a lack of education, jobs and healthcare. But how can fair trade help?

Millions of people across the world live in great poverty.

FIGHTING POVERTY

Trade can bring job opportunities and lead to better education and healthcare services.

In South Korea, for example, the amount of goods and services sold to other countries has increased a great deal. The average person in South Korea is nine times richer than they were 35 years ago.

Help from other countries

Foreign aid can help at first, but the money eventually runs out. In contrast, trade tends to raise more money on a long-term basis.

If poorer countries exported more, many of their people could escape poverty.

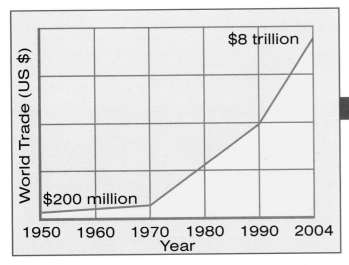

Since the end of the Second World War, trade has risen dramatically. More goods and services are now traded than ever before.

GROWING TRADE

Trade has increased a great deal in the last 50 years. Since 1945, trade has improved standards of living in many parts of the world. As trade increases, the wealth of individuals and nations also grows.

Miracle growth

China has recently become a lot richer because of trade. Between 1980 and 2000, China's economy grew by an average of ten per cent a year. The average Chinese person now earns six times more than they did 20 years ago.

Winners and losers

Although trade is growing, not everybody has benefited. Over one billion people still survive on less than US$1 (50 pence) a day. Nearly eleven million children under five die each year from preventable illnesses, such as measles.

Developing countries are trading more than ever before. Countries like Hong Kong (right), China and Mexico have experienced a fast growth in trade. However, the people who make goods in Mexico have not really benefited. Instead, the sellers make the most money because they add costs for packaging and transportation.

7

Global warming

Scientists estimate that 700 tonnes of carbon dioxide are released into the air every second. Most of this gas is produced by world trade. A build-up of carbon dioxide in the atmosphere could cause the climate to change. If trade continues to increase, the impact on our planet and on us could be very serious.

The environment must be protected from the effects of trade.

ENVIRONMENTAL COSTS

Fuels power factories and vehicles, which help us to trade. An increase in trade means an increase in the use of fossil fuels, such as oil. These fossil fuels are running out.

8

Poverty

Poverty is being hungry and having no home. It is also being sick and not being able to see a doctor. Poverty is having no job or not being able to go to school. Trade can help to reduce poverty because it aids economic growth. This benefits the poor.

Human trade

The slave trade began in the late 1400s. People were sold at markets in Africa and taken by ship to the Americas. They were forced to work on cotton, tobacco, rice and sugar plantations in the Caribbean, Brazil and what is now the USA. Up to 28 million people were sold as slaves until the trade was stopped in the mid 1800s.

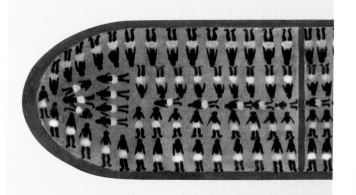

SUPERMARKET GOODS

Next time you're in a supermarket, have a think about where all the food comes from. The shelves of most shops are filled with foods from all over the world. This food may travel thousands of kilometres. But how do we know if it has been produced using fair trade?

The bananas at your local supermarket could be from the West Indies.

SUPERMARKETS

Supermarkets have a lot of control over the supply of food around the world. Supermarkets are able to use their power to get a good price. These deals are not always fair, but they keep prices low for customers.

Encouraging trade

Every day of our lives, we use different products. We eat a bowl of cereal, buy a pair of shoes, or watch a television programme. Each time we buy something, we're telling the people who supply a product that we like it, need it or want it in our lives.

CHOCOLATE

Chocolate is made from cocoa beans. Today, almost two million tonnes of cocoa are produced every year. Chocolate companies like Cadbury Schweppes, Hershey and Rowntree have their products in most supermarkets. The Ivory Coast in west Africa produces over half of the world's cocoa.

A bitter trade

At the end of the 1990s, a United Nations (UN) report showed that some Ivory Coast farmers forced children to work in cocoa fields. Newspaper reports and television programmes claimed that the children worked in poor or dangerous conditions.

Some of these children had been taken from other countries in west Africa. Human rights groups claimed that this was a type of modern slavery. The US imports over US$240 million worth of cocoa from the Ivory Coast every year. It is likely that some of this chocolate is linked to child labour.

A bigger picture

At the same time, cocoa prices were very low around the world. The Ivory Coast's prime minister said that companies would have to pay farmers a better price for cocoa, in order to stop child labour.

Cocoa is often the only source of income for farmers. Companies should pay a fair price for it.

Keeping prices fair

Today, cocoa prices have returned to normal. West African governments and chocolate companies have promised to work together to end child labour.

10

■ This diagram shows how the cost of a jar of coffee is shared between different people. You can see how little the grower receives.

Exporter gets 10%

Coffee grower gets 10%

Retailer gets 25%

Shipper and roaster get 55%

THE PRICE OF COFFEE

The price of coffee beans changes daily. Like other goods, the price of coffee is affected by 'supply' and 'demand'. If there are more coffee beans one year, coffee will be cheaper. But if more people drink coffee, the price will rise.

Between 2000 and 2004, coffee prices fell by over 50%. This is mainly because more countries are producing coffee than ever before. But it means that some coffee growers are becoming poorer.

Price protection

The wellbeing of any country depends on the supply of food. This is why the European Union (EU) made an agreement called the Common Agricultural Policy (CAP). This agreement tries to guarantee a minimum price for farmers, by providing 'subsidies'. Farmers are given money if they grow a particular crop.

Winners and losers

Not all European farmers benefit from the £30 billion agricultural subsidies given every year. Large farms get more money than small farms. Large farms are then able to buy new, efficient equipment and can produce food more cheaply.

11

EXTRA FOOD

Dairy farmers in Europe receive billions of euros from EU governments to produce products such as milk, butter and yoghurt. Farmers are paid for what they produce, but it may be more than Europeans want. Extra quantities can be sold very cheaply in other parts of the world. Europe also produces too much sugar which is sold cheaper elsewhere than at home. But is this fair?

Dumping

'Dumping' is when extra supplies are sold cheaply. This can have a damaging effect on an economy. Sugar farms in Mozambique, for example, had to sack staff in order to compete with new prices. People without jobs spend less money and other areas of the economy suffer.

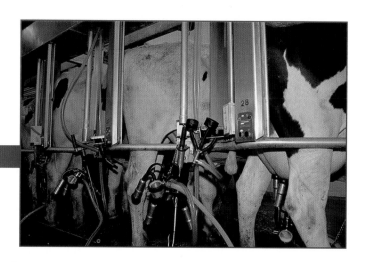

Countries that produce just one or two products will suffer if other countries start 'dumping'.

Lunch in the UK

Next time you have a meal, think about where your food has come from.

Potatoes from Italy

Chicken from Thailand

Carrots from Spain

Broccoli from Zambia

Peas from Zimbabwe

Cabbage from Britain

FAIR TRADE IN CLOTHES

The clothes industry makes about £175 billion a year. Fashion companies are keen to advertise their products to make money. Companies search for cheaper ways to make clothes. They want to keep prices low for customers, to stay competitive.

Moving around

In the last 30 years, the clothing industry has moved from countries like the UK and US to places like China and Bangladesh. Wages are low in these countries, so companies can keep their costs down. They make more money, but workers in richer countries have lost their jobs.

A DYING INDUSTRY

Since the 1970s, thousands of people in Europe have lost their jobs in the clothing industry. Marks & Spencer is one of the UK's biggest clothing companies. It used to source 90% of its clothes from the UK. Now their clothes are manufactured outside Europe. This has been good news for the economy of other countries stretching from Morocco to south-east Asia.

Too long for too little

Today, most of the world's textiles are made in China. However, factory workers complain of long hours and unsafe conditions.

14

Hundreds of mills and factories have closed in Europe.

Clothing factory workers are often treated badly for little pay.

In many factories around the world, workers are forced to do overtime. In most cases, the reward for these long hours is still not enough for workers to support their families.

Working conditions

Workers in these clothing factories say they are treated badly by their employers. They have been called names and sometimes physically abused. It is difficult for the workers to complain because they don't want to lose their jobs.

Chemicals in factories

Factory workers in eastern Europe and south-east Asia often have poor health. Eye damage, back pain and allergies are common. In 2003, the European Union banned a number of chemical dyes because of health concerns.

Cotton is made into fabric in factories all over the world.

In west Africa, farmers grow cotton to make jeans and T-shirts. They are often ill because of the pesticides they use. Some farmers cannot afford to buy protective clothing. Every year, up to 20,000 deaths in poorer nations are linked to the use of pesticides.

Benin, in west Africa, also grows and sells cotton. The money from cotton has helped to build new schools, roads and hospitals. However, the government in Benin does not support cotton farmers. Farmers have to reduce prices if they are to compete with US cotton farmers. If US and Benin cotton farmers were treated equally, Benin cotton farmers could make a better living and contribute more to the economy of their country.

15

COTTON COUNTRIES

In the US, cotton farmers receive money from the government. They will always get a good price for their cotton. This means that US farmers can sell cotton at very low prices, but still make money.

Welsh mining

Coal was once used to power vehicles and for industry. South Wales used to produce a third of the world's coal. Today, however, the coal industry has gone and unemployment is high.

ELECTRONICS AND GEMS

We are using more electronic equipment than ever before. Over a billion homes have a television, over a billion people use a mobile phone and over 600 million people use the internet. But none of this would be possible without the metal tantalum.

FROM THE EARTH

Tantalum is the metal used in electronic circuit boards. It is found in a type of rock called columbite-tantalite, or coltan. Coltan is so valuable that it is known as 'black gold'.

The cost of coltan

Around £3 billion of coltan is sold every year. Because coltan is needed for electronic equipment, it has become very expensive. Some people try to buy coltan illegally. In central Africa, the coltan trade is often controlled by violent groups who use the money they make to buy illegal weapons. These weapons are then used in a civil war.

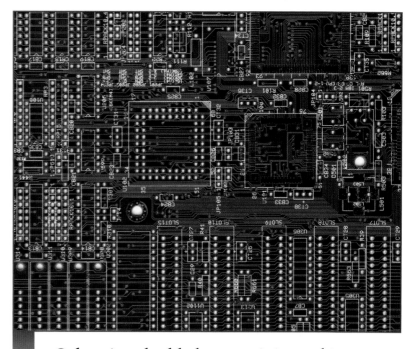

Coltan is valuable because it is used in electronic circuit boards. It is legally mined in Canada, Australia and Brazil.

The threat to gorillas

Over the last 30 years, there has been a lot of violence in central Africa. This has caused the movement of a large number of people.

This movement and the demand for coltan has put great pressure on wildlife in this region. Forests have been cleared and rivers have been polluted. Gorillas have been killed and sold as 'bushmeat'.

The natural environment in central Africa is being harmed by coltan mining.

Safety

As it is illegal to mine coltan in the national parks of central Africa, safety regulations are often ignored. In February 2002, 36 coltan miners were killed when a riverbank collapsed on them.

Coltan and mobile phones

Mobile phone companies say they do not use coltan from central Africa. However, it is often hard to tell where coltan comes from.

The diamond trade also has its problems (see page 18).

17

SRI LANKAN GEMS

Today, around 80% of the blue sapphires we buy come from Sri Lanka. This business is worth about £45 million. Around 175,000 people work in the industry. However, sapphire sellers earn more money than the people who dig for the gems.

In 2003, there were serious floods in Sri Lanka and many people were killed. Illegal digging for gems was thought to be the cause of the swelling rivers. Unless things change, more floods might happen.

CONFLICT DIAMONDS

Diamonds are a sign of love and luxury. However, some diamonds come from parts of the world controlled by military groups. These groups fight against their government. They use the money from diamonds to buy weapons for civil wars. This is common in west and central Africa.

Some people in west and central Africa are killed for their diamonds. Some of these diamonds end up in jewellers' shops in developed countries like the USA (below).

Jewellery is very expensive. However, the people who dig for gems are paid very little money.

THE ARMS TRADE

In 2003, bombs were dropped in Monrovia. This is the capital of Liberia in west Africa. The bombs had been made in Iran and then illegally supplied by a neighbouring country called Guinea. This meant that the weapons got into the wrong hands.

ILLEGAL ARMS

Illegal activities are often funded by the sale of illegal weapons. These include kidnapping, murder and gun crime. Today, technology makes it easier to trade. This is good when products are legal, but can cause problems if they are illegal.

Every year, legal weapons worth £15 billion are sold. Unfortunately, some of these weapons end up in the wrong hands.

Weapons and war

In western Sudan in 2004, an armed group known as 'Janjaweed' started to attack people. Over a million people have now fled their homes in the Darfur (a region the size of France or Texas). They are living in terrible conditions in refugee camps.

EU countries and the US are not supplying Sudan with weapons anymore. But uncontrolled trade has meant that people around the world have access to small weapons. As trade in weapons increases, the price drops. More people can afford to buy weapons. This can be very dangerous.

LEGAL ARMS

In the last 40 years, the number of countries making weapons has doubled. Eight million small weapons are now made each year. It is difficult to keep track of weapons, however. Many weapons are sold in parts rather than as whole weapons.

It is illegal for British companies to sell weapons to some countries in Africa. This is because of the civil wars there. However, weapons are still reaching these countries.

Weapons sold to one country, may end up in another.

Legal difficulties

It is impossible to know where weapons will eventually be used. Around 30 Canadian helicopters were sold to the US, for example, but ended up in Colombia. This is a country in South America with a history of violence.

20

The alternatives

• In 1999, South Africa spent £3 billion on defence. The same money could have treated five million people with HIV/AIDS for two years.
• If governments halved their spending on defence, every child in the world would be able to go through primary education.

FAIR TRADE IN MEDICINE

Every one of us is unwell from time to time. When we are ill we can buy medicine, visit our doctor or get treatment at a hospital.

Many people in developing countries (right) can't afford the medicines they need to get better.

However, poverty means that a third of the world's population does not have regular access to affordable healthcare.

TOO EXPENSIVE

Forty million people around the world have HIV/AIDS. The medicine used for HIV/AIDS can cost £7,500 a year per person.

In South Africa, five million people have HIV/AIDS. But if the average yearly income in South Africa is around £5,000, how can they afford these drugs?

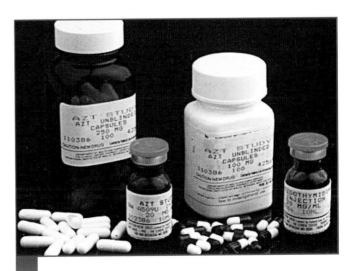

Medicines are often too expensive for the people that need them most.

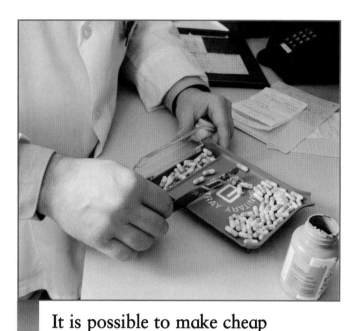

It is possible to make cheap medicines. However, this can cause problems for buyers and sellers.

Cheaper medicine

An Indian company called Cipla can make HIV/AIDS medicine for £175 per year. The medicine is almost exactly the same as the more expensive types. This means that millions of people can afford the drugs.

In 2001, the South African government was taken to court for buying this HIV/AIDS medicine from Cipla. The companies who first made the HIV/AIDS drugs said that the South African government and Cipla were acting illegally.

Future research

It costs a lot of money to research and develop new medicines, so drug companies have to protect their profits. Although an international law makes it illegal to copy their medicines, drugs earn so much money that this illegal trade continues.

The five biggest pharmaceutical companies often make sales of over £10 billion each a year.

22

Copyright

After the South African example, aid agencies such as Medecins Sans Frontieres said that laws should not stop people getting important medicines. Many pharmaceutical companies dropped their court cases.

People felt that health was more important than trade agreements. Governments are now trying to get cheaper medicines for the people that need them.

Essential medicine

In November 2001, a world trade conference agreed that cheap HIV/AIDS drugs should be made readily available.

Governments are now allowed to buy cheaper copycat medicines when there is a public health crisis. These drugs could help in the treatment of an HIV/AIDS epidemic, for example.

Bigger picture

The World Health Organisation (WHO) has found that most medical research helps the richest 10% of the world's population. Between 1975 and 1997, only 13 of 1,223 new medicines were for diseases found in developing countries.

Because of this problem, the Global Health Fund began in 2002. This was meant to be a worldwide fund for medicine to help everybody. However, after two years, the Global Health Fund did not have enough money to really help the people that needed it.

23

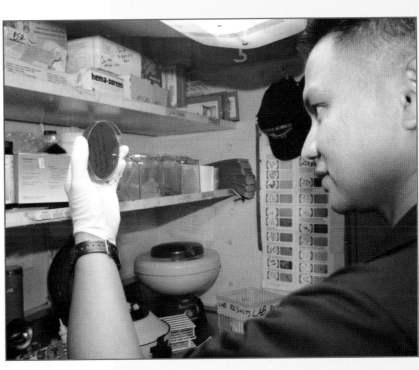

ILLEGAL DRUGS TRADE

Over 50 million people around the world regularly use illegal drugs. Governments spend billions of pounds every year treating addicts and trying to stop the illegal drugs trade.

Governments try to stop drugs coming into their country.

WORLD NETWORK

Today, advanced technology means that illegal drugs move faster and more easily around the world than ever before. Cocaine is mainly produced in South America. It is taken to the US and towards Africa and Europe. Synthetic drugs, such as Ecstasy, are mainly made in Europe. But they are sold all over the world.

24

Making cocaine

Coca is the raw material used to make cocaine. It has been grown in South America for thousands of years. Coca leaves are sold for making coca tea which is legal to drink. However, it is illegal to grow and sell coca as the drug cocaine. Some farmers grow drug crops to make more money. Subsidies in Europe and the US are making it more difficult for some farmers (see page 11). This makes growing illegal crops even more tempting.

BIG BUSINESS

It is not unusual for drug dealers to be arrested at airports or border crossings. These people are taking drugs to cities and towns around the world.

But drug dealers don't control the drugs trade. They are moving the goods for a group of people who work for drug 'barons'. Trading illegal drugs is a business. Highly qualified professionals are used.

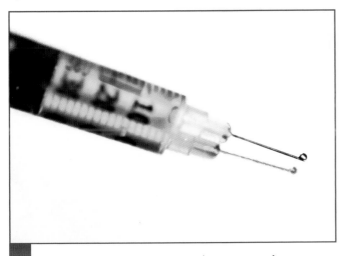

The HIV virus can be spread by sharing dirty needles.

Human cost

The illegal drugs trade ruins millions of lives every year. People who use drugs can become addicted. They may also commit crimes to pay for the drugs they need. Millions of people suffer.

In Vietnam, two-thirds of the people who have HIV/AIDS use illegal drugs.

MAKING DRUGS LEGAL

The problems of illegal drugs have made some people ask whether we should be doing more to stop the illegal drugs trade. Some people think that drug-related illness and crime could be reduced if some drugs were made legal.

If heroin users were given heroin, they wouldn't have to rely on crime to pay for their drugs. Drug users could also have access to free, clean needles rather than using needles that may be infected with HIV. This could help to stop the spread of HIV/AIDS around the world.

25

THE MONEY ISSUE

Developing countries often need money from richer countries and organisations. However, debt is a problem. What happens when a poor country can't pay back the money it owes?

NORTH AMERICA

SOUTH AMERICA

MOVEMENT OF MONEY

In the early 1990s, a lot of foreign money was spent in south-east Asia. People thought this money would help the economy of countries such as Thailand to grow.

However, although there were lots of new buildings, Thailand's economy wasn't doing very well. When foreign businesses realised there was a problem, they began to take their money away.

Within 18 months, most of the foreign money had disappeared. People became nervous about paying for projects in south-east Asia. This caused a social disaster across this part of the world.

The European Union (EU) is the world's largest trading bloc (see page 35). The EU trades throughout the world. However, sometimes the EU trades less fairly with countries who aren't involved in the EU.

China is the fastest-growing economy in the world. China's imports jumped by 40% in 2003. This caused other economies in the region to grow. China is starting to import more from countries in the region.

EUROPE

ASIA

MIDDLE EAST

AFRICA

South Asia is the second fastest-growing region in the world. However, it is also one of the poorest.

India is now one of the largest economies in the developing world.

Economic growth in some parts of Africa is often below 3% a year.

In 2001, £3.4 billion of foreign money was spent in Africa. However, this was mainly in the oil-exporting countries.

AUSTRALASIA

27

Rebuilding lives

By the end of 1998, there was a lot of unemployment across south-east Asia. The economy in this region was suffering. Governments could no longer pay for important services such as

health and education. Loans of £69 billion were given to the south-east Asian governments. Many Asian countries are now doing a lot better. However, Indonesia is still suffering.

In 2001, the people of Argentina were angry. They felt that their government had made the country very poor.

ARGENTINA'S CRISIS

During the second half of the 20th century, Argentina was run by governments who handled the economy very badly. They caused massive unemployment. Around 15 million people were forced to live in poverty.

In late 2001, the government failed to pay a £66 billion loan repayment. The Argentinian people were not allowed to withdraw more than £400 a month from their own bank accounts. People were angry and worried about losing their life's savings.

A new beginning

By the start of 2002, the president of Argentina had been replaced five times in just two weeks. In 2003, Nestor Kirchner became president and things in Argentina began to improve. By 2004, the people of Argentina were less angry. However, there was still the ongoing problem of massive, unpayed loans.

The causes of the debt

South American countries borrowed money in the 1960s and 1970s in order to develop their countries. This is what led to Argentina's debt crisis. The experience of Argentina, Brazil and Uruguay show that old debts continue to cause problems for developing nations today.

Countries in Africa spend around £20 million a day to pay back debts. This gives them less money to spend.

28

FREE TRADE DISPUTES

Free trade means that nothing can stop goods or services moving in and out of a country. Sometimes, governments help their own industries by making it more difficult for foreign goods to be imported. They add costs (tariffs) to foreign goods so they are more expensive to buy.

Governments try to protect their industries against foreign imports.

TRADING NATIONS

Since the Second World War, international organisations have been set up to support and encourage trade between nations.

Bank loans

The IMF (see page 46) was set up to make the world's economy more stable. The IMF lends money to governments. The World Bank also lends money. However, it is involved in longer-term projects. These include building new factories and roads or improving education and healthcare.

In return for the loans, countries are asked to trade freely with other countries. However, as foreign imports increase, local industries can't compete and they have to close down. This has made the debt crisis worse in many developing countries.

A century of trade

In the 19th century, the standard of living in western Europe and the US improved. Many nations became wealthier. Trade was one of the reasons for these changes in people's lives.

Many people had a very good standard of living in western Europe and the US in the 19th century.

The Great Depression

In 1929, the US stock market in Wall Street collapsed. This had a serious effect on the world economy that lasted for ten years. Many countries tried to protect their local industries from outside competition.

Never again

At the end of the Second World War, the governments of Europe and the US needed to rebuild countries affected by war. Trade was a way to build economies and to make the world more peaceful.

New organisations

Towards the end of the Second World War, a number of international organisations were set up. These tried to rebuild countries. Countries also came to an agreement, called GATT. This aimed to make trade rules to improve relations between countries. GATT led to the World Trade Organisation (WTO) (see page 46).

30

In 1999, a WTO meeting in Seattle, USA, failed to agree on many issues.

DISPUTES

Members of the World Trade Organisation (WTO) have to follow WTO rules when they trade. If member countries have a disagreement about trade, the WTO sorts it out.

Keeping trade free and fair

In 1999, up to 50,000 people got together outside a WTO meeting in Seattle, USA. They were angry with the WTO for being secretive about the way it settled trade disputes. People wanted WTO meetings to include other organisations (such as trade unions and environmental and human rights groups). People also argued that the WTO should vote in a fairer way.

The WTO

The WTO headquarters are in Geneva, Switzerland. Since the WTO started in 1995, 150 countries have become members. The WTO uses a system of trade rules to get countries to trade freely and to improve their economies. Every rule tries to encourage free trade – whatever goods or services are being bought or sold.

CANCUN, 2003

Four years after Seattle, a WTO meeting in Cancun, Mexico, also failed. Angry people gathered on the streets of Cancun. However, inside the meeting an even bigger dispute took place. West African countries complained about unfair cotton subsidies (see page 11).

Changes in world trade are affecting the jobs of US steel workers.

Common complaints

The US argued that steel and textile factory workers were losing jobs because of changes in world trade and EU tariffs. Farmers in South Korea were also complaining about rice dumping forcing them out of business.

The trade talks collapse

The WTO meeting ended when people representing the African countries walked out. They argued that developing countries were forced to trade freely when richer countries were not prepared to do the same. They accused rich nations of being unfair because they used subsidies and tariffs that made it more difficult for countries to trade.

A rich man's club

Some people thought the Cancun talks were a success for poorer nations. It was the first time that developing countries had challenged the EU and the US. They argued that the WTO was a club that helps richer nations instead of helping free and fair trade.

Other people were disappointed when the talks ended. They argued that the world needs the WTO to improve difficult trade rules and to stop trade wars (see pages 35-36).

Some WTO rules:

TRIPS

TRIPS are rules which try to protect the money that companies use to research new ideas. TRIPS can make medicines and technology more expensive for poorer nations. However, TRIPS have been successfully challenged. In South Africa, for example, TRIPS rules were overturned in favour of public health (see pages 21-23).

MAI

In 1995, some large companies in developed countries wanted the WTO to make it easier for them to invest in other parts of the world. They wanted the WTO to agree to a Multilateral Agreement on Investment (MAI) to give international companies more power when they invested in foreign countries. However, some people did not like the idea of an MAI. They thought that it made companies too powerful. The WTO has not yet made a decision about an MAI.

GATS

Services such as banking and healthcare are covered by the General Agreement on Trade in Services (GATS). This makes it easier for companies to invest in services. Investment can lower prices and improve services in some cases. However, it can also increase prices and cause poor quality of services in areas such as health and education.

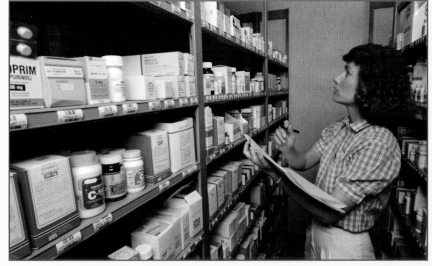

Pharmaceutical companies took the South African government to court when it supplied cheap medicines. However, they did not win the case.

DROP THE DEBT

The World Bank and IMF are not always popular. People argue that because poorer nations have to make changes to get a bank loan, their debt just gets worse.

In 1996, the World Bank and IMF decided to reduce foreign debt repayments in 42 countries. The World Bank, the IMF, richer nations and other organisations agreed to cancel US$100 billion worth of debt over several years.

The outcome

In 1996 a campaign was started by an organisation called Jubilee 2000. They argued that the debt relief process was too slow. They wanted debt cancelled in more countries.

However, debt relief is working. Education and healthcare have improved in ten African countries. Although debt relief is slow, it is a step in the right direction.

Many developing countries could be helped if their debt repayments were cancelled.

TRADE WARS

Countries often sign agreements (or 'trade blocs') with each other. This is to encourage free trade. However, there have been a number of disputes known as 'trade wars'.

BANANA SPLIT

One of the biggest trade disputes was about bananas. A group of fruit-selling companies in the US complained about EU tariffs. They were also supported by five South American banana-exporting countries. The tariffs were used to help banana-growing countries in Africa and the Caribbean.

Settling the war

The US fought back by putting large tariffs on EU imports into the US. This meant that many businesses in the EU suffered. The WTO claimed that the EU had broken some trade rules.

The 'banana war' is over. However, farmers in the Windward Isles are still suffering.

The EU eventually changed its policy. However, many people have not recovered from the 'banana war'. Without money from the EU, many banana growers in former colonies are now going out of business.

The US and the EU had a steel 'trade war' when US tariffs were added to foreign imports.

STEEL WAR

In 2002, the US government put tariffs on steel imports. This was to protect the US steel industry from cheaper foreign imports. The EU and eight other steel-producing countries complained to the WTO. The tariffs were declared illegal.

The US wants to keep subsidies on US cotton.

Fighting back

The WTO said the EU could fight back by putting equal tariffs on US imports. Meanwhile, the US complained to the WTO about another issue. They accused Europe of not using genetically modified (GM) crops. This made trade relations between the EU and US even worse.

Tariffs dropped

If the EU had used tariffs against the US, the amount of imports from the US to the EU would have fallen. This would have caused unemployment in the run-up to the 2004 US presidential election. President Bush dropped the US steel tariffs to protect his presidency. This wasn't very popular with some people.

CANCUN COTTON WAR

Brazil complained about US cotton subsidies at the Cancun conference in 2003 (see page 32). The WTO found that the US was acting illegally in most cases because it caused dumping (see page 12).

A big step

This was the first time a developing country has won a major trade dispute at the WTO. In 2004, the US government said it would fight  back. The dispute over cotton is set to continue. Although some people will lose, others will gain.

LARGE COMPANIES

Foreign money can improve the standard of living in a developing country.

Large companies are very powerful. Their size and number have changed the patterns of trade around the world. They have also helped economic growth. Investments can change standards of living. But if they are withdrawn, it can be a disaster.

COMPANY WORKERS

Large companies make up 70% of trade around the world. But they only employ around 17 million to 26 million people. A lot more people are indirectly employed, however. Companies like IBM or Nike give work to factories which are not owned or managed by them. Nike employs 20,000 people directly. However, over 500,000 people around the world make Nike products. Because so many people are involved, human rights and environmental issues are often a problem.

Winners and losers

Reports of environmental damage or human rights abuse make us ask whether companies are really helping their host countries. Although sales figures show an increase in the economy, it isn't very easy to measure the real costs and benefits to a country.

The environment

Prawn farmers in Indonesia have lost their income. This is because waste from an oil refinery is pumped into the ocean where they fish.

Who makes the clothes you wear?

Some people think that relaxed environmental laws in poorer countries attract foreign companies. Punishing companies who pollute the environment is one way to try to make them more responsible.

Human cost

38

Foreign investment doesn't always improve people's standard of living. Factory workers in China or Bangladesh, for example, suffer poor health.

It is difficult to know who to blame for human rights abuse or environmental damage. Some people argue that cultural differences and the standard of a country's government affects working conditions.

Other people say that deadlines put too much pressure on factory owners and their employees. If a company doesn't get its own way, there is always the worry that it will take its business elsewhere.

Trying to help

Some companies are trying to help, however. Levi Strauss has a factory in the Dominican Republic in the Caribbean. It offers a day-care centre for its workers. It also provides education programmes.

Mind the GAP

Many people stopped buying clothes from GAP because their factories were said to have poor working conditions. Soon GAP produced a new 'code of conduct' for its workers. However, some people think that working standards should be decided by the people who work in factories. Or alternatively, by the governments of those countries.

A LIVING WAGE

More people would have a better standard of living if they were paid fairly. People should be able to afford basic needs such as food, housing, healthcare and education. We must pay a fair price for the goods we buy.

Goods have to be sold at a fair price if workers are to improve their standard of living.

Free trade zones

Governments can also create free trade zones (FTZs) inside the borders of their own country. The Mexican government started an FTZ during the 1960s. This allowed US companies to import goods without paying tax. In return, companies employed Mexicans and exported their goods out of Mexico. As a result, by 2000, the Mexican economy gained US$18 billion.

Some people argue that FTZ workers are exploited and the environment damaged. They also argue that US companies benefit most, taking more profits than the community who makes the goods.

FAIRTRADE

As we become more aware of the problems of world trade we are changing the kinds of products that we buy. Products labelled as 'FAIRTRADE' help to guide us in the choices we make.

WHAT IS 'FAIRTRADE'?

FAIRTRADE helps buyers and sellers to trade in a way which benefits everyone. FAIRTRADE producers are found in poor areas of the world. They receive a fair price for their work. This covers their costs and earns them a living.

Labelling

Foods that are produced under FAIRTRADE terms have a label. In the UK, the Fairtrade Foundation's consumer label (the FAIRTRADE mark) shows whether a product meets strict FAIRTRADE standards. TransFair USA is the only independent certifier of FAIRTRADE products in the US.

FLO (Fairtrade Labelling Organisations International) also recognises more than one million growers in 60 countries. FLO inspectors visit farms to see whether they've met FAIRTRADE standards. Today there are over one million small-scale producers worldwide involved in FAIRTRADE.

The UK FAIRTRADE mark (top left) and the US FAIRTRADE logo (left).

For use not profit

Towards the end of the 19th century, new organisations called 'Co-operatives' started in Europe. Groups like the Co-operative Wholesale Society in Britain re-invested the money they made. Members of the 'co-operative' traded goods and services with one another.

The FAIRTRADE label was started in 1989 by the Max Havelaar Foundation in the Netherlands. This encouraged other FAIRTRADE organisations. In 1991, Oxfam, Traidcraft, Twin Trading and Equal Exchange started a company called Cafédirect. Cafédirect is now the UK's largest FAIRTRADE hot drinks company. Cafédirect also produce FAIRTRADE tea and chocolate.

BUYING WISELY

Most people choose to buy products for taste and price. But you may also want to know how a product has reached the shops. Some people pay more if it means that communities benefit and no unnecessary damage is done to the environment.

Some people think that the FAIRTRADE movement is not realistic. They say that most people are more concerned with saving money so they can go on holiday or buy a new car.

41

Fairtrade has transformed the lives of some coffee farmers. They now earn more money and work in a safer environment.

Slowing down

Some people argue that the growth in FAIRTRADE will soon slow down. They think that FAIRTRADE products will only sell in rich nations where people are able to earn a living. They argue that the FAIRTRADE movement is too small to make any real difference to the billion or more people living in poverty.

More rules

There are also doubts about how much small producers benefit. FAIRTRADE helps communities involved in 'co-operative' groups. But what about other people?

Producers and suppliers have to meet certain standards to be part of a FAIRTRADE network. But some argue that these rules make it difficult for people to benefit from trade.

However, by helping farmers to make a living, FAIRTRADE does help producers to have more control over their lives.

A Ghana tale

Today, nearly 45,000 farmers work for Kuapa Kokoo, a cocoa farming co-operative in Ghana. Kuapa Kokoo was set up in the early 1990s, to allow growers to benefit from exports of cocoa.

In 1998, Kuapa Kokoo started its own FAIRTRADE chocolate bar with a UK company. Kuapa Kokoo's farmers own a third of The Day Chocolate Company. They share the profits and contribute to how the company is run. The profits have helped to buy new farm equipment and to build new wells.

42

Profits from tourism in poorer countries can be re-invested in schools and healthcare.

BETTER INVESTMENT

Companies are now looking for fairer ways to invest. In 1976, the Grameen Bank in Bangladesh began lending money to farmers who had no chance of getting a bank loan. Now more banks are rethinking how they invest in poorer nations.

In 2000, the oil company Shell began investing in small businesses in Uganda that used renewable energy. They decided to invest over £225 million in a long-term project that funded fruit farmers and honey growers to invest in solar power.

WORTH TRYING

The FAIRTRADE movement has increased people's awareness of the difficulties of world trade. Buying FAIRTRADE products is unlikely to reduce the gap between rich and poor countries overnight. However, governments and companies are under pressure to consider the problems of unfair trade. People's attitudes are changing. But powerful groups also control whether more people will benefit from world trade.

CHRONOLOGY

150 BC-1500s AD – The Silk Road joined east Asia, the Middle East and Europe. Materials such as gold, silk and wool were carried along this route of about 6,400 km.

1492-1504 – Christopher Columbus began making journeys from Portugal across the Atlantic. He found the Caribbean Islands. On his third and final voyage he reached South America. This encouraged other European sailors and traders to explore the oceans of the world.

1500-1800 – Vasco da Gama's explorations of western India encouraged more European traders to search for wealth overseas. Trade increased as the explorers travelled further. The influence of European religion and political power around the world also increased.

1765 – James Watt improved the design of the steam engine. This encouraged Nicholas-Joseph Cugnot to make a steam carriage that travelled on roads in France. In 1904, Richard Trevithick also made the first steam train to work on a railway in England.

1876 – Alexander Graham Bell invented the telephone. This was the start of long-distance telephone communication.

1896 – Guglielmo Marconi invented wireless communication which led to the development of the radio.

1860-1945 – By the end of the 19th century, Europeans turned to Africa in search of natural resources. These were needed to support the growing wealth and population in Europe after the Industrial Revolution.

1919 – Arthur Brown and John Alcock flew the first aeroplane across the Atlantic. By the 1920s, airlines began to carry mail. Soon, non-stop flights over oceans and continents became possible.

44

1944 – At the Bretton Woods meeting, the US, the UK and the former Soviet Union had talks with 44 other countries. They wanted to create a stable and peaceful economy after the Second World War. They agreed to set up the IMF and the International Bank for Reconstruction and Development (which later became the World Bank).

1947 – The first international trade meeting was held in Geneva between 23 nations. These meetings are now called General Agreements on Tariffs and Trade (GATT).

1970s – A sudden rise in oil prices meant that many developing countries had to borrow from banks in western Europe. This is where the debt crisis in many nations started.

1983 – The internet was created. This revolutionised communication and banking in the late 20th century.

1989 – The first FAIRTRADE label was launched by the Max Havelaar Foundation in the Netherlands.

1999 – People protested against globalisation and capitalism in Seattle, USA. The demonstrations led to an increased awareness of the problems of trade. These issues included poor working conditions, environmental problems and inequality around the world.

2004 – The charity Oxfam opened a coffee chain in the UK that sold only FAIRTRADE products. One of its coffee brands – Cafédirect – raised £5 million when shares for the company were sold on the London Stock Exchange.

2006 – Attempts at reaching a world trade agreement failed following disagreements between the US and Europe over farm subsidies. Talks continued in 2007 in an attempt to find a solution.

45

ORGANISATIONS AND GLOSSARY

Cafédirect
www.cafedirect.co.uk

Cafédirect is the UK's largest *Fairtrade* hot drinks company.

Fairtrade Foundation
www.fairtrade.org.uk

The Fairtrade Foundation reports on *Fairtrade* issues. It sells *Fairtrade* goods and also sets *Fairtrade* standards.

Human Rights Watch
www.hrw.org

Human Rights Watch investigates and protects human rights around the world.

International Fair Trade Association
www.ifat.org

A worldwide group of over 160 *Fairtrade* organisations. The group works in more than 50 countries.

International Monetary Fund (IMF)
www.imf.org

The IMF monitors the world's financial systems. It also lends money to governments if needed.

Oxfam International
www.oxfam.org

Oxfam is a charity that campaigns on global issues. It supports development projects around the world.

Traidcraft
www.traidcraft.org.uk

Traidcraft is a group that tries to encourage changes in trade rules to make them fairer.

TransFair USA
www.transfairusa.org

A non-profit organisation that certifies *Fairtrade* products in the US.

United Nations Conference on Trade and Development (UNCTAD)
www.unctad.org

A United Nations group that discusses trade and development issues. It helps poor countries to grow and trade with developed nations.

World Bank
www.worldbank.org

A group of organisations who give money and advice to poor countries. This helps them to develop their economies and to reduce poverty.

World Trade Organisation (WTO)
www.wto.org

An international organisation that creates trade rules to encourage fair trade between its members.

Arms – Weapons. Small arms are weapons, such as guns, that can be carried by a person.

Carbon dioxide – A gas given out when we breathe. It is also produced when fossil fuels are burned.

Civil war – A conflict between different groups within a country.

Debt – Money owed to another individual, organisation or country.

Demand – The amount of goods or services that are needed.

Developing countries – Countries that are becoming industrialised.

European Union (EU) – An economic and political group of 27 European countries.

Exports – Goods or services that are sold to another country.

Fossil fuels – Fuels formed from the remains of ancient plants and animals. Examples are coal, oil and gas.

Genetically modified (GM) crops – Naturally grown crops that have been altered using technology to grow faster or to resist pests.

Human rights – The basic freedoms that all humans should have.

Imports – Goods or services that are bought from another country.

Investors – People who put money into businesses to make more money.

Pesticide – A chemical product used against pests that feed on crops.

Stock market – The place where company stocks and shares are bought and sold every day. Stocks and shares can be bought as an investment or sold to make money.

Subsidy – Money given by a government to help a person or a particular group. Farmers are often given subsidies to encourage them to grow certain crops.

Supply – The amount of goods or services that are available.

Tariffs – Costs added to goods and services that are imported into a country. Governments add tariffs to foreign imports to protect their own industries. Also known as duty tax.

Trade unions – Organisations that support the rights of workers.

INDEX

48

Photo Credits:
Abbreviations: l-left, r-right, b-bottom, t-top, c-centre, m-middle
Front cover, 2bl, 9tr, 10mr, 40bm, 41bm, 42br — Transfair USA. 1mc, 4bl, 6bl, 7br, 15tr, 21c, 26bl, 27bm, 28br, 32ml, 35 both, 37tl, 38mt, 40tr, 44tr, 45tr — Flat Earth. Front cover ml, 1ml, 3tr, 4tr, 12ct, 13b, 14bl, 17c, 17br, 18bl, 19bm, 20br, 24br, 25tr, 29br, 30ml, 34b, 37c, 39tl, 43t, 45bl — Corel. Front cover mr, 1mr — Jonas Jordan/Courtesy of the U.S Army. 2-3b, 5mt, 7ml, 8bl, 11br, 12mlt, 13tr, 14tr, 16tr all, 17tl, 21tl, 22 both, 23br, 31c, 31br, 33 all, 38mr — Corbis. 5mr — Sony Ericsson. 6tr — Peter Manzelli/USDA. 8tl, 18br, 19tr, 25ml, 31t, 39ml, 42mt — Photodisc. 9br, 44bl — Ken Hammond/USDA. 11tl, 28tl, 39br — Select Pictures. 12mrt — Bill Tarpenning/USDA. 12mlb, 12mrb, 12bl, 12cb, 12br — Stockbyte. 15ml, 36tr — John Deere. 16br — Ingram Publishing. 19c — PFC Joshua Hutcheson/Courtesy of the U.S Army. 20t — SPC Jason Heisch/Courtesy of the U.S Army. 21br — NIH. 23tl — Médicins Sans Frontières. 23br — Tommy Gilligan/U.S. Navy. 24tr — Robin Ressler/USCG. 29tr — James Tourtellotte/U.S. Customs & Border Protection. 30br — Dorothea Lange/USDA. 36br — European Parliament. 40cl — Fairtrade Foundation.